A TRUE BOOK™

Australia and Oceania

MEL FRIEDMAN

Children's Press®
An Imprint of Scholastic Inc.
New York Toronto London Auckland Sydney
Mexico City New Delhi Hong Kong
Danbury, Connecticut

Content Consultant
Susana Lei'ataua,
Asian/Pacific/American Institute
New York University
New York, NY

Library of Congress Cataloging-in-Publication Data

Friedman, Mel.
  Australia and Oceania / by Mel Friedman.
        p. cm. -- (A true book)
  Includes bibliographical references and index.
     ISBN-13: 978-0-531-16866-0 (lib. bdg.)
              978-0-531-21828-0 (pbk.)
     ISBN-10: 0-531-16866-2 (lib. bdg.)
              0-531-21828-7 (pbk.)
1. Australia--Juvenile literature. 2. Oceania--Juvenile literature.
I. Title.

  DU96.F75 2008
  990--dc22   2007048064

Produced by Weldon Owen Education Inc.

1 2 3 4 5 6 7 8 9 10 R 18 17 16 15 14 13 12 11 10 09

Find the Truth!

Everything you are about to read is true *except* for one of the sentences on this page.

Which one is **TRUE**?

T or F   Australia's largest cattle farm is bigger than the state of New Hampshire.

T or F   The peoples of Papua New Guinea speak about 300 different languages.

Find the answers in this book.

Contents

There are an estimated 20,000 to 30,000 islands in the Pacific Ocean.

The Pinnacles Desert is in Western Australia. It features thousands of limestone pillars.

CHAPTER 1

Down Under

About one-third of Australia is desert.

Australia, the smallest of Earth's seven continents, is nicknamed Down Under. That is because it is below the **equator** on a standard world map. Australia lies entirely in the Southern **Hemisphere**, between the South Pacific Ocean and the Indian Ocean.

Equator

Southern Hemisphere

Australia

Indian Ocean

South Pacific Ocean

Dry Earth

Australia is mostly low and flat. In its center is a vast region called the Outback. This is an area of desert and dry grasslands. Australia's only mountainous region is along the east coast. It is called the Great Dividing Range, or Eastern Highlands. The highlands are moist and fertile. Other parts of Australia face serious droughts. Even under normal conditions, many Australian rivers and lakes dry up for part of every year.

In most years, hot, dry winds help spread wildfires throughout Australia. The fires destroy forests, animals, and homes.

Australia

Torres Strait

Darwin

Northern Territory

Pacific Ocean

Great Barrier Reef

Great Dividing Range

Indian Ocean

Western Australia

Queensland

South Australia

Great Dividing Range

Brisbane

New South Wales

Perth

Adelaide

Sydney

Canberra

Victoria

Melbourne

Tasman Sea

Tasmania

Hobart

N W E S

Sunny States

Australia is divided into six main states, as shown on the map. The states along the north and west of the continent are warm all year round. In the south and east of the continent, winters can be cool. The southeast coast receives regular rainfall and sometimes snow.

Seasons in the Southern Hemisphere are opposite to those in the Northern Hemisphere. Summer is from December to March. Winter is from June to September.

The frilled lizard lives in forests in northern Australia. It displays its neck frill to frighten predators.

CHAPTER 2

Awesome Animals

Australia is an isolated land mass surrounded by water. Animal life there developed separately from that on other continents. This has given Australia some of the world's most unusual creatures. There are many kinds of reptiles, including about 500 species of lizards and about 140 species of snakes.

Koalas rarely need to drink. They get the water they need from the leaves they eat.

Weird and Wonderful

Australia's distinctive animal groups include its marsupials (mar-SOO-pee-uhlz). These are mammals that begin life in their mother's belly pouch. Wild kangaroos, koalas, and wombats are marsupials found only in Australia. Kangaroos, the biggest of them, can be as tall as six feet (1.8 meters). They can hop as fast as 30 miles (48 kilometers) per hour. However, they cannot go backward!

A baby kangaroo is called a joey. A joey spends its first six to eight months growing inside its mother's pouch.

Platypuses are expert swimmers. They use their large bills to scoop up worms and shellfish from streambeds.

Australia also has the only egg-laying mammals in the world. These are the platypus (PLAT-uh-puhs) and the echidna (i-KID-nuh). Echidnas look like hedgehogs. They are also called spiny anteaters.

Australia has about 700 species of native birds. The flightless emu is related to the ostrich. It is the largest bird in Australia. Emus can run as fast as kangaroos.

A kookaburra call sounds like human laughter. ➡

Coral on the Great Barrier Reef

Stunning Sea Life

The Great Barrier Reef is a chain of more than 2,000 **coral reefs**. It is the world's largest reef system. The reef stretches along Australia's northeast coast for about 1,240 miles (2,000 kilometers). It provides shelter for thousands of kinds of fish, dolphins, sea turtles, and sponges. Human activity and climate change are among the threats to this delicate **ecosystem**. The Great Barrier Reef is now a protected area.

Baaa!

Many farms in the Australian Outback are used for raising cattle or sheep. These large farms are called stations. Many stations cover more than 1,000 square miles (2,590 square kilometers). The largest cattle station in the world is Anna Creek Station in South Australia. It covers about 9,142 square miles (23,677 square kilometers). That's larger than the state of New Hampshire!

Sheep are raised for their meat and wool. Australia is the world's largest wool producer. Men who work on cattle and sheep stations are called "jackaroos." Women are called "jillaroos."

Red Rocks

In the middle of the Australian Outback is a group of gigantic rocks with caves inside. Some of the caves have rock paintings that are about 40,000 years old. This area features in creation legends of the Aborigines (ab-uh-RIJ-uh-neez), Australia's earliest people.

Kata Tjuta and Uluru

Kata Tjuta (The Olgas)

Kata Tjuta (KAT-a tuh-JOO-tah) means "many heads." The area is made up of 36 dome-shaped rocks. The tallest dome is 1,791 feet (546 meters) high.

Uluru (Ayers Rock)

Uluru (OO-loo-roo) is one of the biggest freestanding rocks in the world. It measures about 1.5 miles (2.4 kilometers) long and 1,142 feet (348 meters) high. It also extends 1.5 miles (2.4 kilometers) underground!

Aboriginal paintings often tell stories of the Dreamtime. Each dot or line represents a person, an object, or an animal.

CHAPTER 3

Australia's Past

Aborigines migrated from Southeast Asia at least 50,000 years ago. Aboriginal culture is the oldest uninterrupted culture in the world.

Aborigines name the beginnings of the world and of knowledge as the Dreamtime. They believe everything on Earth was created in the Dreamtime by songs sung by the ancient spirits.

Aboriginal dot paintings were originally made in the sand or on bark.

Finding Food

Aborigines are expert at living off the land. Some still live in the traditional way, hunting

Boomerangs have been used for hunting, digging, fighting, and even as musical instruments.

and gathering much of their food. They hunt with clubs, spears, and boomerangs (BOO-muh-rangz). A boomerang is a flat, bent piece of wood. It returns to the thrower if spun into the air. A hunter can easily kill a small animal with one well-aimed fling of a boomerang.

Aborigines also gather seeds, fruits, nuts,

Witchetty grubs are popular bush tucker. Some people say that they taste like peanut butter!

and insects. This diet of native plants and animals is known as bush tucker. (In Australia, *bush* means the countryside, and *tucker* is another name for food.)

Making Music

Traditional music and dance are important in Aboriginal culture. Children are encouraged to sing and dance from a young age. They are also taught dances depicting Dreamtime legends. For these traditional dances, Aborigines paint themselves with earth and plant dyes. Some dances represent birds or other animals. Each community or clan passes stories between generations within the family.

Aborigines invented the didgeridoo (DIJ-uh-ree-doo), one of the oldest wind instruments. It is made from a hollow tree branch.

Sailors and Jailers

Europeans did not settle in Australia until the late 1700s. The Dutch mapped it in the 1600s but did not stay. Then, in 1770, British explorer Captain James Cook landed in what is now Botany Bay, Sydney. He claimed the land for the British Empire.

In the late 1780s, Britain set up a **penal colony** in Australia. The prisoners built roads and buildings. Conditions were very harsh. Many prisoners were sentenced to life terms. If not, and they survived, prisoners were free to start new lives in Australia. Most were not allowed to return to Britain.

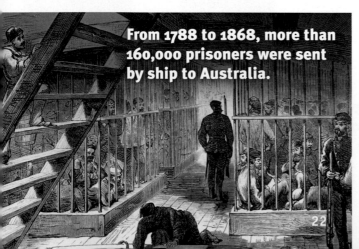

From 1788 to 1868, more than 160,000 prisoners were sent by ship to Australia.

Some people were sent to Australia for petty crimes, such as stealing a loaf of bread.

22

Land of Riches

From Australia's early history, one industry affected its population more than any other—mining. When the gold rush started in California in 1848, many Australians rushed there to seek their fortune. Stores and farms were simply abandoned. Then, in 1851, gold was discovered in Australia. Miners poured into the land down under. The population more than doubled in ten years.

In the late 1880s, opals were found in New South Wales. **Immigrants** arrived from all over the world. Today, the country produces about 95 percent of the world's opals.

Opals are precious gemstones. They contain a rainbow of colors. The black opal, shown here on the left, is the most valuable kind.

Chinatown is a lively neighborhood in the city of Sydney. Chinese immigrants settled there during the gold rush of the 1860s.

CHAPTER 4

Modern Times

Australia has a very **multicultural** society. More than 20 million people live there. About 80 percent are of European descent. Only about two percent are Aborigines. Most Aborigines now live in cities. A growing number of Australians are recent immigrants from India, China, and Southeast Asia.

As in Britain, Australians drive on the left side of the road. ➔

DRIVE ON LEFT IN AUSTRALIA

In the Air

People living in the Australian Outback are far from cities. Still, they have access to great medical care and education. The Royal Flying Doctor Service was established in Australia in 1928. When people in remote areas get sick, the flying doctors provide emergency medical care.

Schooling is provided in the Outback by Schools of the Air. Children stay at home to go to class! Teachers give lessons using two-way radios, video conferencing, faxes, and the Internet.

A School of the Air

Children as young as seven years old can learn lifesaving skills and enter junior competitions.

In the Water

Many Australians love water sports, such as swimming, surfing, and sailing. It's not surprising that Australia has led the world in beach safety. Surf Life Saving Australia has been patrolling beaches and saving lives since 1907.

Australians speak English, but they use many slang words.

Australian Slang	Meaning
Oz	Australia
Aussie (OZ-ee)	Australian
Gidday	short for "Good day"
nipper	young surf lifesaver
shark biscuit	new surfer
togs/cozzie	swimsuit
hard yakka	hard work
mate	friend
beaut/bonzer	excellent

27

The Palau islands in Oceania
include more than 200 coral reefs.

CHAPTER 5

The Vast Pacific

North and east of Australia is the Pacific Ocean, the largest ocean in the world. As many as 30,000 islands are scattered over millions of square miles of water. This vast region is called simply the Pacific Islands, or Oceania. Australia and Oceania overlap each other. Together, they cover more than a third of Earth's surface.

The peoples of Papua New Guinea speak about 860 different languages!

This Papua New Guinea man has painted his face for a ceremonial dance.

Islands Galore

Oceania is divided into three main areas. Melanesia lies to the north and east of Australia. North of Melanesia are the tiny islands of Micronesia. The islands of Polynesia fall within a huge geographic triangle made by New Zealand (Aotearoa), Easter Island (Rapa Nui), and Hawaiʻi. Hawaiʻi is the only U.S. state that is not in North America.

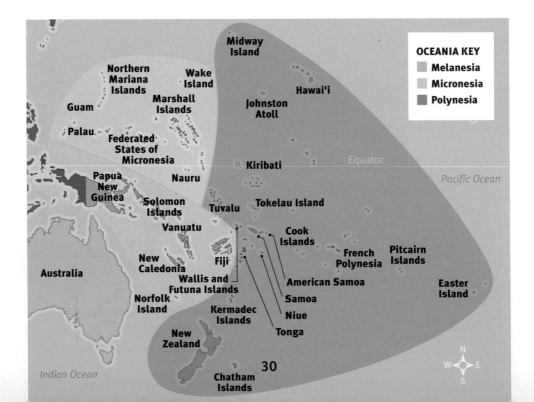

OCEANIA KEY
- Melanesia
- Micronesia
- Polynesia

Midway Island
Northern Mariana Islands
Wake Island
Hawaiʻi
Guam
Marshall Islands
Johnston Atoll
Palau
Federated States of Micronesia
Papua New Guinea
Nauru
Kiribati
Equator
Pacific Ocean
Solomon Islands
Tuvalu
Tokelau Island
Vanuatu
Cook Islands
French Polynesia
Pitcairn Islands
Australia
New Caledonia
Fiji
Wallis and Futuna Islands
American Samoa
Easter Island
Norfolk Island
Samoa
Kermadec Islands
Niue
New Zealand
Tonga
Indian Ocean
Chatham Islands

30

N W E S

The Na Pali Coast on Kauai Island, Hawai'i, is known for its sheer cliffs.

High Islands and Low Islands

There are two kinds of islands in Oceania: high and low. High islands, such as those of Papua New Guinea and New Zealand, have rugged mountains and volcanoes. The highest island mountain in the world is Mauna Kea, in Hawai'i. It rises about 33,000 feet (10,000 meters) from the ocean floor.

Low islands are either eroded volcanoes or coral-reef **atolls** (A-tawlz). Atolls are built up by coral deposits over millions of years.

Hot and Cool

Much of Oceania lies within the **tropics**. There are two seasons—the wet and the dry. Oceania's low islands are usually hot and dry. They have no rivers and little rainfall. New Zealand is located farther south. Its climate is mild and has four seasons.

The winds in parts of Oceania can be extreme. Strong winds and heavy rains often create huge tropical cyclones, called typhoons. Each year, typhoons blow down houses and trees. Many people lose their lives.

Cyclone in Hawai'i

Cyclones in the Southern Hemisphere spin clockwise. North of the equator, they spin counterclockwise.

Ring of Fire

Volcanic eruptions or earthquakes occur when forces build up between Earth's **tectonic plates**. At the edges of the Pacific Ocean is a zone called the Ring of Fire. More than half the world's active volcanoes are located in the Ring of Fire. So are about 80 percent of the world's earthquakes.

White Island, New Zealand

Walk on the Wild Side

Papua New Guinea, the largest island in Oceania, is a lively place. It is covered with tropical forests, grasslands, and swamps. Crocodiles and snakes are abundant. Some animals are related to those from nearby Australia. For example, tree kangaroos and echidnas live on Papua New Guinea. There are thousands of bird species. The southern crowned pigeon, the world's largest pigeon, is from Papua New Guinea. One of the world's smallest parrots, the Red-breasted Pygmy parrot, is also a native.

Papua New Guinea's Queen Alexandra's birdwing is the largest butterfly in the world. Its wingspan can reach 11 inches (28 centimeters).

New Zealand's weta (WEH-tah) is a huge insect. Its body length can reach four inches (10 centimeters).

Natives and Newcomers

New Zealand lies far from any other Pacific island. Before the arrival of humans, some 1,400 years ago, the only residents were lizards, frogs, bats, insects, and birds. New Zealand has no snakes. In the 1800s, European settlers arrived. They brought many other animals, including cattle and sheep. Today, the country has more than 40 million sheep!

The kiwi is a flightless bird that is native to New Zealand. It is the only bird that has nostrils at the end of its bill.

Nostrils

Melanesians have been living in Vanuatu for about 3,000 years.

CHAPTER 6

Island People

The Pacific Islands were settled at various times. It is thought that Papua New Guinea's first inhabitants came from Southeast Asia about 50,000 years ago. About 1,200 years ago, Polynesians called the Maori (MOU-ree) canoed to what is now New Zealand. They **navigated** using only the wind, stars, ocean currents, and birds as guides.

The Maori name for New Zealand is Aotearoa. It means "land of the long white cloud."

Land of the Giants

The **indigenous** peoples of Hawai'i and Rapa Nui (Easter Island) are also Polynesians. They were farmers and fishermen who worshipped many gods as well as their ancestors. Without metal tools, the earliest settlers of Rapa Nui carved hundreds of giant statues out of stone. Some of these statues stand as high as 40 feet (12 meters). Much about them remains a mystery.

Oceania Time Line

About 50,000 B.C.
People from Southeast Asia begin to travel to Oceania by canoe.

800 A.D.– 1350 A.D.
The Maori come from eastern Polynesia to settle in New Zealand.

Divide and Rule

In the late 1800s, Britain, France, Germany, and the United States took control of much of Oceania. Diseases they brought wiped out the whole population on some islands.

During World War II, many Pacific islands were the sites of bloody battles. After the war, many islands became independent nations. Others have remained territories of Australia, New Zealand, the United States, and France.

1000 A.D. – 1650 A.D.

Giant statues are erected on Easter Island.

1768 – 1779

Captain James Cook explores Australia, Tahiti, New Zealand, and Hawai'i by sailing ship.

Craft and Culture

Traditional crafts are still made throughout Oceania. People use plant fibers to weave baskets, mats, and clothing. They make tough cloth from strips of pounded tree bark. The cloth is then rubbed with plant dyes.

Carvers work in wood, bone, and shell. Some carvings tell stories of the past.

Pacific peoples have oral traditions, not written languages. Histories and knowledge have always been passed along through stories and art.

Maori wood carving, New Zealand

Celebrating Art

In every nation in Oceania, a different language is spoken. Each culture also has its own music, art, and dance styles. One way of seeing many cultures in one place is at the Festival of Pacific Arts. Once every four years, a different country in Oceania hosts the event. More than 25 Pacific countries participate, showcasing their traditional and contemporary arts.

Tivaevae (tee-VIE-vie) is an art form from the Cook Islands. Women work together to make colorful patchwork quilts entirely by hand.

41

Island Life

There is a range of lifestyles in Oceania. On many of the islands, people live in villages. They fish and grow their own food. However, in New Zealand, more than 70 percent of the people live in cities. The main crops on low islands are coconuts and bananas. The high islands have more diverse crops and industries, such as mining and timber. In Oceania, as in Australia, traditional cultures thrive alongside a modern way of life. ★

Products from coconut trees include food, medicine, oil, soap, fertilizer, fiber, building materials, and even mosquito repellent!

True Statistics

Population of Australia: About 21 million

Area of Australia: 2,978,147 square miles (7,713,364 square kilometers)

Number of kinds of Australian marsupials: More than 130

Highest recorded temperature in Australia: 123.3°F (50.7°C) in Oodnadatta, South Australia, 1960

Population of Oceania: About 15 million

Number of languages spoken in Oceania: About 1,200

Did you find the truth?

T Australia's largest cattle farm is bigger than the state of New Hampshire.

F The peoples of Papua New Guinea speak about 300 different languages.

Resources

Books

Arnold, Caroline. *Easter Island: Giant Stone Statues Tell of a Rich and Tragic Past.* New York: Clarion Books, 2004.

Bartlett, Anne. *The Aboriginal Peoples of Australia* (First Peoples). Minneapolis: Lerner Publishing Group, 2001.

Bergin, Mark. *You Wouldn't Want to Travel With Captain Cook!: A Voyage You'd Rather Not Make.* New York: Franklin Watts, 2006.

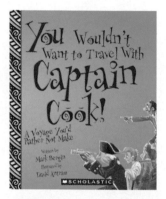

Di Piazza, Francesca. *New Zealand in Pictures* (Visual Geography). Minneapolis: Lerner Publishing Group, 2005.

Greig, Charlotte. *Oceania* (Cultures and Costumes). Broomall, PA: Mason Crest Publishers, 2002.

Fowler, Allan. *Australia* (Rookie Read-About Geography). Danbury, CT: Children's Press, 2001.

Olson, Nathan. *Australia: A Question and Answer Book.* Mankato, MN: Capstone Press, 2005.

Theunissen, Steve. *The Maori of New Zealand* (First Peoples). Minneapolis: Lerner Publishing Group, 2002.

Organizations and Web Sites

Boomerangs

www.boomerangs.org/how.html
Learn how to throw and catch a boomerang safely.

Kids Down Under

www.gigglepotz.com/caustralia.htm
Surf the links to learn about animals and places in Australia.
There are also quizzes, recipes, and an Aussie dictionary.

Wayfinders: A Pacific Odyssey

www.pbs.org/wayfinders
Read about how the Polynesians and Europeans traveled
to, and settled in, parts of Oceania.

Places to Visit

Uluru-Kata Tjuta National Park

Yulara
Northern Territory 0872
Australia
+61 (8) 8956 1100
www.environment.gov.au/
parks/uluru
Take a guided walk to these
amazing rocks and view
ancient rock art.

Wai-O-Tapu Thermal Wonderland

PO Box 1992
Rotorua
New Zealand
+64 (7) 366 6333
www.geyserland.co.nz
In this park, you can
see an erupting geyser,
bubbling mud pools,
and volcanic craters.

Important Words

Aborigine (ab-uh-RIJ-uh-nee) – one of the earliest known inhabitants of Australia, or one of their descendants

atoll (A-tawl) – a ring-shaped coral island with shallow water in the center

coral reef – a large area where the skeletons of tiny sea creatures have built up to form a home for other sea life

ecosystem (EE-koh-siss-tuhm) – a community of animals and plants interacting with their environment

equator – the imaginary line around the middle of Earth, halfway between the North Pole and the South Pole

hemisphere (HEM-ihs-fear) – half a sphere; either the half of Earth above the equator or the half below the equator

immigrant (IM-i-gruhnt) – a person who comes from abroad to live permanently in a country

indigenous (in-DIJ-uh-nuhss) – the original people living in an area

multicultural – having many cultures

navigate – to find a way through

penal colony – a place where criminals are sent to live

tectonic plate – one of the large slabs of rock that make up Earth's outer crust

tropics – the hot areas of Earth near the equator

Index

Page numbers in **bold** indicate illustrations

About the Author

Mel Friedman is an award-winning journalist and children's book author. He holds a B.A. in history from Lafayette College and four graduate degrees from Columbia University, including one in East Asian studies. He has written or co-written more than two dozen children's books, both fiction and nonfiction. His other True Book titles include *China*, *Africa*, and *Antarctica*. Mel often works on projects with his wife, who is also a writer. They have a grown-up daughter.

PHOTOGRAPHS: Big Stock Photo (© Andreas Meyer, back cover; Moorea Mountains, p. 5; p. 12; kookaburra, p. 13; boomerang, p. 20; opal on right, p. 23; p. 31; p. 34; p. 37); Digital Vision (p. 7); Getty Images (p. 8; p. 22); © Harvie Allison/www.harvpix.com (surfers, p. 27); istockphoto.com (p. 3; p. 6; p. 14; black opal, p. 23; p. 25; p. 32; canoe, p. 38; Captain Cook, p. 39; p. 40); More Images/FLPA (platypus, p. 13); Photodisc (Easter Island statues, p. 39); Photolibrary (front cover; p. 10; pp. 15–18; witchetty grubs, p. 20; p. 21; p. 24; p. 26; p. 33; kiwi, p. 35; p. 36; p. 42); Stock.XCHNG (p. 11; weta, p. 35); Stock.Xpert (p. 43); Tranz/Corbis (woman, p. 5; p. 28; p. 41)